FACE TO FACE

FACE TO FACE

BARBARA BENJAMIN

Barbara Benjamin

Nepperhan Press
Yonkers, NY

2009
Nepperhan Press, LLC
Yonkers, NY 10702

First Edition

Printed in the United States of America

Library of Congress Control Number: 2009925496

ISBN: 9780979457944

Cover painting by Barbara Benjamin

For Andrew David,
who always does his best to live face to face

ACKNOWLEDGMENTS

In the two decades between the publication of my first volume of poetry, *Through My Window*, and the writing and publication of this volume, many of the friends who supported my earlier efforts have passed on. They remain a part of my life and all their kindnesses and all we shared together still enrich my days and sustain me. This volume vibrates with their memories: David A. Lowry, Felicia Gizycka Magruder, Edmund C. Spencer, John P. McMahon, and Gail Varnberg. My mother, Ruth Abelson, passed on at the age of 92 and her love endures as a source of my strength.

Since her death over a decade ago, my godmother, Marie Fairon-Lancelot, lives on as my spiritual guardian and her powerful and miraculous intercession continues to grace my life.

Other friends remain, and I am grateful for a lifetime of support from Eileen Curran Bopp, Karen Weinstein, and Teddy Cameron. I am particularly grateful to Father Joe Girzone, the shepherd of my soul. His courage and faith inspire me and make my journey possible.

I have also been abundantly blessed with new friends who encourage and validate my work: Sister Claude Marie, Father Richard Rohr, Carol Diskus, Cathy Bell, Kathie Karl, Orest Bedrij, Tom Milton, and Father Philippe Charles.

Marie Milton kindly agreed to proofread the manuscript, and I am especially thankful for her diligent and expert work.

I am grateful, above all, to a generous, patient, and loving God who has brought all these blessings into my life.

When I was a child, I spoke as a child, I understood as a child, I thought as a child: but when I became a man, I put away childish things. For now we see in a mirror dimly, but then face to face. Now I know in part; then I shall understand fully, even as I have been fully understood.

1 Corinthians 13:11-12

CONTENTS

FOREWORD

I just finished reading the poems in *Face to Face* by Barbara Benjamin. At first I read each poem rapidly because they read very rapidly, but I soon realized that I was missing so very much that was hidden in each line of each verse. Then I started reading them a second time and meditated on each description in every line. To my surprise, I experienced something I had not experienced in my life before. I found each of my five senses come alive.

I could see the living trees and flowers and tree frogs, and all the moving creatures in the lively world of nature in the author's fertile mind. I could not only see with my eyes, but I could also hear the bullfrogs and smell the musty bog that was their home. I could hear the varied songs of birds in trees and hear the drops of rain falling on the leaves of newly burgeoning leaves and fiddlehead ferns, and against a window pane. I could not only see the sun, but could also feel the warmth of its rays against my forehead, even sitting in a dark room in my house. When the verse described raspberries, my tongue could taste their tartness as if I had just picked them to eat.

And the poems are not only about the miracles and wonders of nature; they also penetrate the world of the mystics:

> I wear your cross inside me,
> Like my skeleton of love,
> So different from the dry, bare bones
> I keep warm inside my glove.
>
> I live your cross inside me;
> It integrates my being:
> Where pain abides, there's also joy;
> Where I was blind, I'm seeing.

The author's range of meters and words is both powerful and playful. Some poems are like snow crystals falling like feathers on a soft white blanket; others, like horses on a racetrack. If you want to have a moving mystical experience, pray these poems. If you want to have just plain fun, browse through these remarkable poems on a bright sunny day, and then meditate on them on a melancholy rainy day. You will never tire of reading this book.

Joseph F. Girzone

HAVE YOU NOTICED RAINY DAYS

Rebirth

Pussy willows round the pond;
Nature's waved her sacred wand;
Rituals of spring return;
Fiddleheads foretell new fern.

Robins busy mending nests;
Day and night, no creature rests;
Life itself must be renewed,
Males beguiled and females wooed.

Listen closely, hear the song;
Problems do not make life wrong;
Take the hope each season brings;
Fill your soul until it sings.

Hear the peepers, hear the frogs,
Serenading in the bogs;
Hear the crisp, undaunted brook
Rushing into every nook.

You can almost hear the earth
Giving way to life's rebirth;
If you really listen well,
You can hear your own heart swell.

A Drop of Rain

A
single drop
of soft spring rain
Tapped upon the window pane;

It
will not
ever tap again,
That gentle, single, drop of rain.

Summer Dawn

Before I saw the sun rise up,
The song birds of the summer dawn
Awoke me from my careless sleep
And lured me toward the day, newborn.

With urgency, in lush-green trees,
With quite a shrill cacophany,
They coaxed me, most emphatically,
To leave my dreams, arise, and be.

And so I rose to greet the day,
And look about my world to see
What simple wonders filled my life,
Now I was truly cleansed and free.

The bittersweet was rambling wild
Among the ripening raspberries,
A promise of an autumn treat,
An earth that never ceased to please.

The sun was rising quietly;
Its light was scattered through the leaves;
A silent star to warm the air
And try to heal the ravaged seas.

A steadfastness beyond my wit,
A faithfulness so pure, so rare,
A challenge to each man alive
To live with love, to dare, to care.

On meadow flowers drenched with dew
And trembling in the soft silk breeze,
Responding to life as it is,
I fell in prayer upon my knees.

Storm Clouds

Day colors change before my wondrous eyes
In torrid afternoons of summer skies;
The azure that defied the blue jay's wing
Gives way to lustrous greys that storm clouds bring.

The whiteness that infused the midday heat
Turns black like midnight near the garden seat;
Above the spot where wisps of clouds dripped cream,
A violet hue invades with threatening gleam.

So bright and dark at once the rain sky looms,
Chiaroscuro sweeping through the rooms;
Behold the special beauty of the storm,
Approaching violence that's belied by form.

While beauty, light, and color fill the air,
There is no time for fear or for despair;
This moment colored grey and purple black
Is lost if I decide to turn my back.

So is it with so many moments rare:
They're only here for me if I will dare
To stop and watch while in a breath of space
I'm favored by the splendor of God's grace.

Bliss

I love to watch the morning rise,
And lie here in my haze;
I love to see clear crystal light
Intensify the days.

I hate to go to fancy shows,
All tinsel and unreal;
I'd rather stay and watch the hawk
Shape spirals while I kneel.

I love to sense the breathlessness
Of children keen at play;
I love to hear that earnestness
With which they speak and pray.

I hate to fill my cocktail time
With gossips and with prattlers;
I'd rather crawl around the brush
And watch for timber rattlers.

I love to smell the hyacinths:
Their fragrance fills the room;
I love to see the spider weave
And watch the house cat groom.

I hate the nods and curtseying,
The uptown smiles and wit;
I'd rather walk and talk with God
And wander off a bit.

I love the lads and lassies,
Weaving through my years,
Their joy, their banter, and their warmth,
Their tenderness and tears.

I'd hate to think reality
Required more than this:
To greet with total willingness
The birth of each day's bliss.

'Twixt Day and Night

A risen moon above the trees,
A waning sun stretched cross the seas;
I look to left;
I look to right;
And there I see both day and night.

And, I, a traveler bound to earth,
Am subject to the heaven's mirth:
A full calm moon;
A bold twilight;
I'm left to figure out the sight.

Good-naturedly, I shall await
Absurdity, which is my fate;
I'll travel on,
'Twixt day and night;
I'll come upon the path that's right.

Until that time, from day to day,
Confusion may well have its way;
And moons will rise
Before suns set;
And I will swim in life's droll net.

Now

Like ballerinas in the breeze,
The fuchsias twirl and bow;
Another summer passing through
The beauty of the now.

A bluebird in the bittersweet,
A sight that's rare to see;
The moment moves into the past,
And we are left to be.

A shy coyote in the woods,
In just a blink, it's gone;
A single thought records the sight,
And so the sight lives on.

In time that is immeasurable
Beyond the mortal clock,
A universe exploded once;
We, now, perceive the shock.

Beauty

Little black-capped chickadees,
Warbling in the winter trees,
The slightest hint of warming sun
Invites them out to have some fun.

Branches of the wildest rose
Glisten with the rain that froze;
Come Cartier; come Tiffany;
Try to compete with what I see.

Every season's special here,
In these woods where truth is clear;
Just let the beauty touch your soul;
In that, alone, you've reached your goal.

My Little Joys

"How do you have such fun?" you asked;
I must thank you for that question;
It helps affirm my gratitudes
For all my playful attitudes.

My little joys from day to day:
The woolly worms and pinwheel games;
The caroling in busy malls;
The poems I write; the wild geese calls.

The giggling with my timeless friends;
The fulfillment of the moments
When your eyes twinkle bright as mine,
And we both know we're doing fine.

The brand new sense each season brings;
The ceaseless sound of roaring seas;
The colors of awakened dawns;
The stillness of the grazing fawns.

My little joys, my daring knights,
Like challengers to all life's plights;
So come along, show me your stuff;
I can take it — my joys are tough.

Canterbury

Claire and I in Canterbury,
Bouncing through the ruins;
Life and death at odds again
In these dismal tombs.

Dare we whisper; dare we smile,
As we bounce along;
Dare we keep our joy intact;
Are we deadly wrong?

Bad enough that Becket died,
And that he was slain;
Bad enough that where he died
Only swords remain.

Bad enough they took his shrine
And defiled his name;
Why must Claire and I, alive,
Play that mournful game?

If God is love, if God is life,
I trust that he assumes
Just why Claire and I rejoice,
Even in the tombs.

Have You Noticed

Have you noticed rainy days:
Some folks run for cover;
I stand there and feel the rain,
Stroking like a lover.

Have you noticed sunny days:
Some folks run for cover;
I stand there and feel the sun,
Warming like a lover.

Have you noticed snowy days:
Some folks run for cover;
I stand there and watch the snow,
Sparkling like a lover.

Have you noticed all God's gifts:
Some folks run for cover;
I stand here receiving gifts,
Knowing God's my lover.

Symbols

Symbols are found;
Symbols abound;
Even our death's just a symbol.

Truth we can see
Is just to be,
Be what we are while we're mortal.

Foolish to ask
What is our task;
Trust is the guidepost of being.

Listen and hear;
Everything's clear;
Wake up and see what you're seeing.

Awakening

I screamed an existential scream
Inside an existential dream;
It left me all alone and scared;
It left me feeling no one cared.

When I awoke, the scream had stopped,
And all my fears had slowly dropped;
And in their place, a loving hand
Was leading me along the strand.

I hope I will not sleep again
Inside that existential pen,
Where life seems lost and meaningless
And I have no sins to confess.

I pray that I can stay awake
And conscious of each small mistake,
So I can be a living part
Of God's eternal, loving heart.

On the Brink

Will you take this soul, my Lord;
I fear you'll find me lacking,
In my strength and in my faith,
And you will send me packing.

Then, my Lord, where will I go,
Where will I find salvation;
I have been just everywhere,
In every railroad station.

You alone have offered hope
And lifted me from daydreams;
You alone have nourished me
And cleansed me in your sunbeams.

Now as I stand on this brink,
Where you can shun or claim me,
I must trust the hope I feel;
I must trust you'll set me free.

Free in love and free in life,
Free to enjoy my story;
Free to be responsible
To your unending glory.

Coming Home

The pain I felt before the light
Was buried deeply, out of sight;
And I could not, with mortal eyes
Reveal my pain, nor see God's skies.

Not nearly living, nor half dead,
My soul was waiting to be wed;
While suitors came and suitors went,
My soul just lingered, gnarled and bent.

How could I know the pain I'd feel
When all the veils began to peel,
And I could stand and make my claim
Upon my God and call His name.

His tender touch and strength and peace;
His covenant that will not cease;
His oneness and His trinity;
His ultimate eternity;

All this and more I know not of
He offers with His boundless love;
And here I stand in tears and pain,
A mortal soul come home again.

Still Shy

I imagine God was looking for me,
While I ran recklessly looking for Him;
I imagine He found it baffling to see
This homeless bird flying from limb to limb.

I imagine God wisely wondering why
I didn't simply stand still under His sky;
I imagine He thought me foolish and wild,
Refusing to be His satisfied child.

I imagine God knows I'm not fully tame,
Still balking and shy when I hear His name;
I imagine He knows His job's not done;
The war's over, but the battle's not won.

Your Cross

I wear your cross inside me,
Like my skeleton of love,
So different from the dry, bare bones
I keep warm inside my glove.

I live your cross inside me;
It integrates my being:
Where pain abides, there's also joy;
Where I was blind, I'm seeing.

I love your cross inside me:
It graces me with wisdom;
It cuts a path of happiness
That leads me to your kingdom.

Sore Loser

The devil that owned me now owns me no more;
He scowls and he glares and he stomps on the floor;
For he's lost his power to lure me astray,
To tempt me with daydreams that don't last a day.

Snug in safe harbors and anchored by caring,
I'm led by white light toward all God's preparing;
While Lucifer, baffled, in brown leather hat,
Paces and wonders why his magic went flat.

Deep Waters

Sail fishing;
Dream wishing;
Would the past could fade.

Fly casting;
Dreams lasting;
It's in the past we're made.

Clam digging;
Old rigging;
It's in the past we stayed.

Deep waters;
Sons, daughters;
We see the past replayed.

Beyond Symbols

Fight over symbols;
Fight 'til you die;
Which tell the truth;
Which tell a lie.

Though they're just symbols,
Though they're just dust,
We forfeit life
Rather than trust.

Somewhere beyond them —
Where we won't see —
All that we are
Waits to be free.

Too Many Gods

Too many gods attending here;
Too many gods, too many years:
The gods of then; the gods of now;
The gods who will or won't allow
The other gods within their space,
The other gods, the other face.

Where is the god of one and all,
The god that answers each man's call,
Without a church or shrine to build,
Without a prayer book to be filled,
Without a need to scrape and kneel,
Without a quarrel at the wheel.

Where is the god who sets us free,
Who does not need a bended knee,
Who asks us only to be true
To what we feel and what we do,
Who worships with us, side by side,
Who loves us all with steadfast pride.

Are we, in fear, denying him,
Forsaking freedom, joyless, grim,
Avoiding wisdom of his ways,
Resisting all our unknown days,
Preferring gods to keep us bound,
Lest we be free, and safe, and sound.

Stonehenge

So now I have seen Stonehenge,
That monument of hope,
Sitting like a huge junk heap
Atop a country slope.

Where love could move a mountain,
Fear has dragged a stone;
Where joy could touch the heavens,
Cold reverence stands alone.

One can see that ancient race
Huddled beneath the sky,
Their prayers entwined with moon tides,
Their fate to live and die.

Yet they were not so different
Than I, now passing by,
My prayers entwined with forces
Beyond my mortal cry.

I wonder when it's over —
This modern world refined —
What monuments of truth
We will have left behind.

Wishful Thinking

If only we would fight ourselves,
And leave the other guy alone;
If only we would look inside
And find our faults and then atone.

If we would just stay home a spell
And clean our corners really well,
Then we would not expect so much
From so and so and such and such.

Then we would surely have enough,
Between ourselves and our own stuff,
To satisfy our deepest need
And quiet all our thirst and greed.

Then we could reach out past our sphere
And welcome others to come near;
And we'd be there when they arrive,
And each and every one would thrive.

Resurrection

Why I lie here, I can't tell,
Listening to the mourning bell;
So much lost and so much found,
Moving forward without sound.

Sensing every anguished soul
Listening to a mourning toll;
Resurrection's in the air;
Some deny it; others dare.

Global warheads turn to peace;
Tribal bigotry to cease;
Before this day draws its shades,
New foundations will be laid.

Can the mortal heart endure
Evolution, swift and pure,
Now upon us, everywhere —
We are called; rejoice in prayer!

Evolution

Ghetto people, black or blue,
Did not have a single clue
What it's like to really be
Living bold and living free.

Bound to habits from the past,
They were victims of their caste;
Real emotions locked away,
Prescribed laughter, prescribed play.

Slowly now, the world comes round;
Tribal customs come unbound;
All God's children have a chance
To evolve past circumstance.

As these changes bring new hope,
Those who can rejoice and cope;
Others, who can't move ahead,
Left behind, in pain and dread.

It's a time to kneel and pray,
As each dawn invokes each day,
Bearing witness to what's new:
How, through time, man's freedom grew.

Solitude

I like being with me this year;
Living's fun without so much fear;
My solitude's a warm, rare gift
That rests my soul, my mind adrift.

The hungry crowds, the careless throngs,
With empty hearts and boring songs,
Filled up my space with all their toys,
And drifted through my life like noise.

Not really friendship that will last,
They came and went; like years, they passed;
Another place for me to hide,
To go along, just for the ride.

Today, I'd rather be alone,
To sense and touch each subtle tone:
The nuances that color dreams;
A quiet love's pervading beams;

A harmony of souls in flight;
A private joy; a private night;
The memories that promise more;
The growth and change deep in life's core.

Impatience

Impatience is a friend of mine;
It never keeps me quite in line;
It hurtles me past boundaries
And lures me toward the cold, deep sea.

A friend like this I hardly need;
I wonder if some nasty deed
Could on this clinging friend befall,
Blindfolded up against a wall!

Or if you'd rather, I could try
This loathsome friend to tar and fry;
There may be other cruel, mean tricks,
Like turning it to candle wicks.

Alas, I fear, that in the end,
One cannot shake off such a friend;
So if you see me scurry by,
You needn't ask me — you'll know why!

Freedom

I no longer have to be
A bit more than I am;
I can cavort and frolic
Like springtime, newborn lamb.

Beyond a sense of safety,
Beyond a sense of peace,
I sense my soul eternal,
Beyond my mortal lease.

I wear life's mantle lightly,
Down to the last detail;
Enjoyment is the measure
By which I pass or fail.

There are no gods before me;
There are no gods behind;
The one God whom I worship
Is everywhere and kind.

My worship is most childlike;
I follow where He leads;
All His bliss and harmony
Inform my words and deeds.

Though some days look like chaos,
While others seem well-planned,
I sense a great adventure
Along life's timeless sand.

Such freedom is exquisite,
And all it asks of me
Is that I be responsive
And live life consciously.

A Poet's Lament

I wonder will there ever be
An end to all this poetry;
It seems to be a bit perverse
To always ramble on in verse.

The great one, Freud, knew no known cure
For saints and poets who endure;
For him such beings stood apart
From all the cases on his chart.

Now Jung embraced the mystic mind,
And, in each one, saw all mankind;
But he became daft and dreary
Following his abstract theory.

So here am I, betwixt, between,
A poet sensitive and keen;
By Freud, ignored; by Jung, adored;
I'm left to seek my own accord.

TO LISTEN IS TO PRAISE

Resonating

The impact
of others,
Their words and their dreams,

The rustling
of autumn,
The sounds of what seems

Like life
plunging forward
To simply be heard,

To share
through our being
The sense of Your word.

Things Grown Old

There is a warmth to things grown old;
Compared to them, new things seem cold:

The chipping paint on time's old chair;
The buckled wood that's proud with wear;

The ancient stream and forest grand,
Protective of the new-tilled land;

The ripened fruit, so soft and sweet;
The readiness of full-blown wheat;

The human mind, the human heart,
That has the wisdom to impart
The hope and love and strength and praise
To guide the children in God's ways.

Summer Porches

Dusk quiets summer porches graced
By tender moments that are traced
In memories of special times,
In lovers' words like soft wind chimes.

Here, hearts can rest in easy chairs
And contemplate their daily cares,
Surrounded by the gentle strife
Of mating birds and woodland life.

Here, all the world seems poised in peace,
A twilight that may never cease,
A stillness that may calm all fear
As new thoughts shaped by night draw near.

The Last Rose of Summer

Harsh winds of autumn whirl about
The deadened bits of memory,
Of summer, ready, verdant, moist,
Promising fertility.

A single rose resists the wind,
Defiant, prickly, proud, and red,
More brilliant now than in its prime,
Familiar patterns scattered, dead.

Upon the topmost branch it sits,
While all around, the mighty trees
Stand barren, ocher, grey, and grim,
Content to yield their drying leaves.

What point to struggle to hold on,
When all you've known is dead and gone;
What secret do you try to share;
What courage do you feed upon.

For weeks, or more, raw, raging rains
Have threatened to destroy your stance,
Each morning rising through such gales
That challenge like a fencer's lance.

I watch intently, loathe to learn
The lesson you so bluntly teach:
That life itself has its own ends,
The ways to which we're forced to reach.

Would you not like to join the rest,
To settle silently in sleep,
Instead of staying captive here,
Among the gardens death has reaped.

For life, not death, holds you so hard,
Expecting much, demanding more;
Though you proclaim your victory,
You too must walk through life's last door.

Race Rock Lighthouse

Grey fog

    drips

        immaculate

           pearls

              of

                vapor

                    over

                  the Race Rock lighthouse,

                    over

                  the eternal stones of time,

luring

      the heart

           into

              ethereal

                forgetfulness,

burying,

      in its opulent veil,

           the rampaging riptide of life.

Never and Forever

Never and forever —
The two extremes of now —
Keep us in a quandary
Where we ask "why" and "how."

Never and forever —
Distortions of today —
Keep us from the challenge
Of finding our own way.

Never and forever
Fill our dreams with dust,
Leave us without pleasure
Because we dare not trust.

Never and forever —
The enemies of peace —
Drop them for a moment,
And watch your worries cease.

Fragments

Someday,
    I will take these tiny
             jig sawed
                  pieces
that I reconstructed
      ever so painstakingly
          from the splintered
               bits of memories,
         from the flavors and aromas
                of fantasies,
      that now fit together

s o   v e r y   p a n o r a m i c a l l y

        and

      collapse them again
        into a
        heap
      and put them
          away on a shelf
             labeled
              "Yesterday!"

But before I do,
I will lovingly remove each piece that forms
the fragile visage of a child trapped forever,
it may seem, amid those fragments of insanity.

Those pieces
I will place with care
in a scrapbook
filled with the snapshots of today,
filled with the color and the warmth
of beauty,
eternity,
and truth.

The Hudson Line

They dropped her off when she was nine,
Somewhere along the Hudson Line;
She did not have a railroad map;
She did not have a warm snow cap;
She had no mittens for her hands;
She had no bows or fancy bands.

She stood there in the freezing cold;
She acted brave; she acted bold;
She bowed her head to hide her tears;
She smiled to quell her aching fears;
She spoke to no one passing by;
She dare not speak; she dare not cry.

She took the first train that came through;
She took a seat as if she knew
She might forever have to roam;
She had no place to call her home;
She was alone to make her way;
She'd be an orphan from that day.

She watched the others on the train;
She spoke to them deep in her brain;
She would not be one of the crowd;
She'd make believe that she was proud;
She could not act like other folk;
She could not laugh; she could not joke.

The train came to its final stop;
She stayed aboard like some lost prop;
She had no special place to go;
She sat there swaying to and fro;
She sat there for an hour more;
She rolled, asleep, onto the floor;

The train again began to roll;
She stayed asleep like some lost soul;
She jerked and tumbled with the ride;
She managed to stay safe inside;
She found a haven for her dreams;
She built a world with private schemes.

Though many years had passed her by,
She's now awake beneath the sky;
She has no memory of the train;
She's been renewed by time and pain;
She feels at home and warm and free;
She does not worry where she'll be.

She knows a love that's pure and true;
She counts her friends more than a few;
She's learned to laugh and play and joke;
She's now like ordinary folk;
She barely knows how she came to;
She only knows there's work to do.

She's happy that she's not asleep;
She's noticed that her soul is deep;
She holds no blame, no cruel despair;
She lives each day with thanks and care;
She's not the girl who once was nine,
Abandoned on the Hudson Line.

Getting Here

I feel my lifetime moving fast,
Absorbed by a voracious past,
With appetite for all that's mine:
My heart, my thoughts, my limbs, my spine.

What yesterday I dreamed and feared,
Today has nearly disappeared;
Those things that I did dare to do,
Today no longer are brand new.

If I let go and live today,
As if there were no yesterday,
I'm guilty of forgetting how
I came to live and love right now.

So I'll not turn my back or sneer
At moments that have brought me here;
But, in my soul, I have professed,
It is right now I love the best.

A Prayer

Here is a place inside of me;
Now is a place I want to be;
You are the force that sets me free:
My soul, my heart, my energy.

Inside my soul is here and now;
Within my heart, my will I bow
To you, my Lord, who leads the way,
To you, my God, who is each day.

Here is your grace, and yours alone,
Giving me access to your throne;
Here is your glory, yours alone;
My life, my time, are just on loan.

Dear Lord, I thank you, full in heart,
For all the gifts that you impart;
Dear Lord, have mercy as I speak;
You alone know the path I seek.

Simply, I pray you use my life;
Simply, I pray to ease the strife,
As we each struggle on our way;
Simply, my Lord, your will I pray.

This Day

You've given me this day to rest,
To contemplate my mortal quest,
To walk the land beneath fall skies,
My Lord, your grace to recognize.

You've given me this day to feel
The endless bounty of your meal,
The taste of love and usefulness,
Of satiated thankfulness.

You've given me another day
To take a chance, to come your way,
To realize my life renews
Each moment that it's you I choose.

Gifts

I live in a world of giving, and then,
The gifts that I give come right back again:
They come back in poems that point me toward dreams;
They come back like wood ducks floating down streams.

I've learned to receive these bounteous gifts
That fall at my feet like soft snow-white drifts;
I've learned to absorb their beauty and light;
I've learned to wake to each day with delight.

I give all I have to balance a bit;
But all that I have is hardly a wit
Of all I receive as I greet each day;
By nightfall, I simply thank God and pray.

Your Love

You love me through your children;
They're scattered through the land;
They reach out and embrace me;
They offer me a hand.

You love me through awareness
Of gifts that you bestow:
They reach to every corner;
They beckon me to grow.

You love me past endurance —
I am a little thing —
Your gifts are vast, eternal,
Beyond my mortal ring.

With wonderment, I thank you,
For your love does not cease;
In gratitude, I follow,
Toward your abiding peace.

Judas Iscariot

I pray that I no longer carry the plate
Of Judas Iscariot, that devil's mate;
For scoundrel like him, I most surely have been,
Betraying my Lord with my unconscious sin.

In truth, there is never a soul here alive
Who doesn't encourage old Satan to thrive,
Choosing, like Adam, to know and control,
To set his own limits and name his own goal.

Carelessly abusing the gift of free will,
We often refuse to just trust and sit still;
Not sensing that while we're misshaping our days,
God uses our straying to teach us His ways.

For the angel God loves above all the rest
Is the angel who puts our souls to the test;
So be thankful for sin and humbly repent;
For the sinner you are is the sinner God sent.

Your Church

Your church is where I find I see
The foibles of humanity;
I see the cross that you must bear;
I see the children in your care.

I gain no solace from that view;
I wonder, dear Lord, how can you?
Or is it quite enough that we
Are being all that we can be?

Have you a vision of the whole,
In which we each play some small role;
And, in that vision, do you see
A turning point in history?

Or do you also suffer pain
When we appear to make no gain,
When we plod on like ancient slaves
Between our infancy and graves.

I never feel quite as alone
As when the throng comes to atone,
And, mindless, as they seem to be,
Provide my soul no company.

And, yet, I like to be with you,
Your ancient rites, each time, renew;
I am attracted to your light,
But I can't simply be polite.

My heart cries out for stronger stuff;
The rites we have are not enough;
Too many people walk away;
Oblivious to grace, they pray.

The world is hungry for real prayer,
The kind of prayer that few men dare,
The kind without a guarantee,
The kind that truly sets men free.

No longer can we live like fools,
In vague obedience to rules;
Our time is now; the path is clear;
Dear Lord, please teach us how to hear.

Uncertain Times

Uncertain people, uncertain times:
Nobody knows for whom the bell chimes;
Once there were chestnut and hickory trees;
After the blight, they're vague memories.

Uncertain people, uncertain times,
Trapped inside of old nursery rhymes:
A frustrated Jack and a thirsting Jill
Trying to climb that unending hill.

Uncertain people, uncertain times:
Isn't it clear for whom the bell chimes?
Your nursery rhymes and old memories —
Victims of blight like old chestnut trees.

You are the people; this is the time;
You now face a new mountain to climb;
Look to each day as you wake to each morn;
Trust the message: you will be reborn.

Directions

You help me to carry my cross
By carrying your own;
You help me help humanity
By being fully grown.

You're a child of mine forever,
But while you are on earth,
You must become all you can be
And live to your full worth.

I have suffered all my children,
But now it's time to know
That you do me grave injustice
If you refuse to grow.

You have within your own creation
The tools that you may need;
You have within your consciousness
The essence of my seed.

If you refuse that consciousness,
If you refuse to know,
You are guilty of destroying
What I, in love, did sow.

Here, I've given you fair warning:
You have a job to do;
I've given you the will to choose —
The rest is up to you!

To Listen is To Praise

As You are mere symbol
That we have created
Of what You truly are,
Then how much more blessed
To be in your Being
When we have crossed the bar.

As You are mere shadow,
Reflection eternal,
A pattern in the light,
Then how much more freeing
To bathe in Your essence
When we are graced with sight.

As You are mere knowledge
That we have constructed,
Like fools, afraid to know,
Then how much more wisdom,
In silence, to listen:
To hear, to praise, to grow.

Charlie McCarthy

Like Charlie McCarthy,
I sit on God's lap;
He pulls the strings;
I start to yap.

And like Edgar Bergen,
He throws out his voice;
I move my mouth
Without much choice.

The spellbound audience
Cannot really see
Who speaks the words
Coming through me.

They just sit and enjoy
My words and my tone;
They do not know
I'm made of bone.

Like Charlie McCarthy,
I sit on God's thighs;
He writes my script;
I seem so wise.

And like Edgar Bergen,
He sits very still;
So it appears
I have free will.

Now would anybody
Who really is free
Spend all this time
Straddling God's knee.

I offer this question;
I have no reply;
This is my life;
I don't know why!

ABUNDANCE IS GOD'S RULE OF THUMB

Change

You cannot catch the mourning dove,
Not even with your eye;
It flits about the monkey pod
And decorates the sky.

You need not catch the mourning dove,
Not even in your mind;
Abundance is God's rule of thumb,
So leave right now behind.

Across the stream of yesterday,
So many doves flew by;
Attempt to clutch them to your heart,
And you and they will die.

Doves darting 'round the throne of life,
Like jesters come to bring
A lesson we are loathe to learn,
That change alone is king.

Paradise

...and man created Paradise
upon a molten rock;
he brought ideas and planted trees,
but he did not take stock
of all the latent fear and greed
that one day would collide
and darken dreams in Paradise
and undermine his pride.

This Paradise man builds on earth
is rarely safe, it seems,
from being reconstructed by
some other fellow's dreams;
until the day man heeds the roar
of Pele cross the seas;
until he finds his Paradise
upon his bended knees.

Flying

They celebrate dawn;
They herald the night:
These feathered creatures
In their noisy flight.

Day means more to them
Than ever to me;
It must be that they
See more than I see.

Man wanted to fly;
Today, that's a cinch;
But he flies a plane;
Ah, that is the pinch.

He still cannot fly
Alone on the wind;
Perhaps that's because
He feels he has sinned.

Perhaps that's because
He really can't see
The light of the world
That sets the birds free.

Grace

Northwesters bend the coco palms
And winter roars with rains
That lash the ocean's boiling tide
And soak the planted plains.

The seas respond in turquoise flames,
Resplendent with pure force,
That flair triumphant on the rocks
And glorify their source.

While we seek shelter from the storm,
And pray the aftermath
Will leave our little worlds intact
And not disturb our path.

On sunny days, it's hard to see
Our simple state of grace;
But when the storm has reached its peak,
Man's truth lies face to face.

Peace

I've walked along the twilight shores
Of my eternity;
I've watched the sands lead me along
Toward where I'm meant to be.

I've slowly followed as the tides
Receded and returned;
I've found new footing on the land,
While undercurrents churned.

I've clearly marked the setting sun,
Behind volcanic peaks,
A molten glow against the sky,
A maiden's blushing cheeks.

I've been informed by where I've been,
And all that I have seen,
That here, on earth, we make our peace,
And sense what God may mean.

Photography

I photographed the world and, then,
I photographed the world again;
And when I finished what I found
Was that I could not capture sound.

I could not hold within my lens
The bubbling morning song of wrens;
I could not focus on the light
That calls the migrant geese to flight.

I could not change my speed to see
The trust and love that sets life free;
And all those things I want to have,
I could not really photograph.

The Dance

You came and said "I love you";
I did not ask you to;
You completely filled and warmed me,
With a love so pure and true.

I quivered as you touched me:
A white winged moth in flight;
You protectively embraced me,
Then released me to the night.

I flew beyond the moment;
I landed in a trance;
I slept till I was called again
To awake and join the dance.

My Faith

My faith is fragile;
Did you think it strong?
Praise heaven, my friend,
You couldn't be more wrong.

It breaks like a twig,
All brittle with frost;
It sways like a mast,
All tattered and tossed.

It creaks like a floor,
Buckled with aging;
It cries like a child,
Frightened and raging.

My faith's so tender,
So soft and infirm;
In truth, it is clear,
I'm God's weakest worm.

I squirm when I sense
The bounty He bears,
When He makes so clear
How deeply He cares.

It takes forever
For me to reply;
When He reaches out,
I'm tongue-tied and shy.

My faith's aflutter,
A hummingbird's wing,
Adrift on the breeze,
Like this song I sing.

Tug of War

You call me forth, and I pull back;
You stroke my soul, and I attack;
You offer hope, and I decline;
You lead the way; I cling to mine.

This tug of war, this battle ground,
This road to you goes round and round;
Each little step, each little turn,
So steep it seems, so hard to learn.

The ego fights; the flesh rebels;
The ghosts hold on inside my cells;
So slow to trust, yet keen to grow,
I'm wary of each seed you sow.

Dear Lord, stay close; invite me near;
Help me to pray; help me to hear;
I am too weak; I am too strong;
Dear Lord, please lead my soul along.

Trust

How anxious, child, you have become,
As if you knew me not,
As if I had not ever touched
Your tiny cosmic dot.

How foolish, child, to hold back trust,
As if I had not shown
My total love for all you are,
Since you were just half grown.

How truly human you can be,
How trivial and crude,
When you deny your destiny,
When you demand and brood.

Yet all I've ever asked you do
Is let me fill your needs,
And trust you'll be rewarded by
The flowering of your seeds.

Abandoned

It's not my fault,
It never was,
That you ran off
Away from us.

Some demons who
Held you as prey
Kept you alone,
Kept you away.

It's decades now
Since you last left;
My infant soul,
In tears, bereft.

It took this long
For me to see:
You did not run
Away from me.

Ghosts

A shadow on the x-ray of my soul,
Old tissues scarred by those who were not whole,
By those who stood as guardians of youth,
By those who had no knowledge of the truth.

A haunting in the chambers of my heart,
Grey ghosts of days that I have set apart,
As I have moved beyond my primal fear,
As I have left behind those I held dear.

A clarity informs the waking day;
Faint shadows of the past now fade away;
Not memory, nor will, nor reverie
Can hold those ghosts the way they used to be.

A readiness to turn away from pain;
A cleansing of the past by drenching rain;
A nurturing of brand new fields of grain;
A blessing to be born to life again.

Yesterday

I have looked into the grim, gaunt face of yesterday;
I have watched the ghosts of then play hide and seek;
I have stood beside the altar of old rituals;
I have seen great, aged kings turn grey and weak.

I have listened to the hollow words of years gone by;
I have talked to those I knew could never hear;
I have waited at the threshold of millennia;
I have paid with stifled dreams the price of fear.

I have felt familiar thoughts pull at my energy;
I have heard the tunes of songs I used to sing;
I have brushed away the clinging dust of memories;
I have been prepared for what this day may bring.

Running Wild

We seek death for warmth and comfort,
To recreate the womb;
We mourn our lost serenity;
We make of life a tomb.

We struggle for our unity
On all the wrong side roads:
The fast lanes and the fantasies;
The social teas and codes.

We medicate our misery
With drugs and love affairs;
We run from our realities
And deepen our despairs.

We look outside for clarity,
While God awaits within;
Abandoning our infant souls,
We live a life of sin.

We give others all our power,
Or seek control of them;
We fragment our perceptions:
The rose, the thorns, the stem.

We order our priorities
To hold onto the past;
We misinterpret all we see,
So only nightmares last.

We manipulate so quickly
That we do not suspect
That we drive joy away from us
And get what we expect.

We wonder why we're unfulfilled
By all that we've achieved;
Deep inside our aching cells,
We know we are bereaved.

We hesitate when trust and hope
Come knocking at our door;
We'd rather not be vulnerable
Where we've been hurt before.

We live in our old memories;
We know no other way;
The past and present all converge
In one unending day.

We hide in places that seem safe;
We rarely take a chance;
We measure our security
By power and by stance.

We cling to all the old dead lies,
The only life we knew;
We demand that strangers certify
Those lies of life are true.

We bury our integrity
In habits of abuse;
We build a storehouse filled with guilt
For all our soul's misuse.

We walk this earth so ego-bound,
We cannot find the sky;
We shun the freedom that is ours;
We'd rather fret and cry.

We are the children of the light;
Yet we choose to deny
The hand of God that waits with love,
If we will only try.

Released

Since that long day that my dad died,
I have been stretched;
I have been tried.

I've been released to seek my fate,
To find my way,
with God, my mate.

I've been convinced by all I see
That my dear dad
returned to me;

That he released my soul to heal,
As I released
him to his wheel;

That in the end, we all are here
To lend a hand,
to love, to cheer,

To nurture souls, as far we roam,
To share the truth
that God is home.

Healing

I've split myself asunder
To make room for your cross;
And all that's left of what I was
Is some vague sense of loss.

You've healed me from the inside;
You sit within my heart;
There is no truth beyond your love;
You are each day's new start.

I know no other purpose
That I am free to seek;
You rule the realm inside of me;
You are the words I speak.

I find your cross no burden;
I find your purpose clear;
I find your healing love a gift;
Dear Lord, I'm glad you're here!

Being Out

Down and out
or
Up and out...

Being out
is
Being out...

Spring

The rites of spring include some snow,
Falling on those seeds I sow;
The newborn day includes the past,
Out of which some memories last.

Perhaps that's why spring jars me so,
Warm and luring life to grow,
Then heedlessly reminding me
Just how cold life used to be.

Counting

We count the money in our bank;
We count how many beers we drank;
We count the hours of the day;
We count how many prayers we pray.

We count to weigh and measure change;
We count to scale a mountain range;
We count to touch the infinite;
We count to know God, bit by bit.

We count to keep our thoughts in check;
We count the trump cards in our deck;
We count the errors that we make;
We count too much for our own sake.

Time

If all I see is some time past,
And what I know I knew,
Then now cannot exist at all,
And time is just a clue.

The motions of a ticking clock
Belie what truth reveals,
That light is born in nothingness,
And action spins life's wheels.

The chronon of the quantum world,
The Cronos of the tales,
Two giants of a different size,
Beside which all time pales.

So here and now and for all time,
I release my measure,
And turn my back on all that counts,
Counting God my treasure.

New Moon

New moon behind the great old oak:
Not new, not old, not really;
That moon was there before that oak,
Before the world, or nearly.

All that is new, all that is old,
Exists outside all reason,
As each of us, in our own time,
Determines our own season.

My life is new; my days are old;
My soul has come a distance;
So for right now, I am quite young;
How old are you, for instance?

Tribal Pride

Fierce tribal pride, like dinosaurs,
Sends up a clashing roar,
Across a globe that now prepares
To let its spirit soar.

In hamlets bound to yesterday,
The clans awake with fear
That all they ever held as truth
Is timed to disappear.

So they fight on as they have fought,
So desperate to control
Those fragments of their fantasies
That make the past their goal.

And we look on, the rest of us,
And watch fatalities
Replacing all their ancient laws
And distant memories.

Until, at last, the earth's at peace,
And each man stands alone,
And offers all he can become
To God, his only throne.

Wild Swans

Wild swans at Westerly,
Like those Yeats saw at Coole;
An ocean doesn't matter much
To a poet or a fool.

Old mariners spout tales,
Like those that Coleridge told;
The centuries repeat themselves,
As God's designs unfold.

The great white whale sounds deep;
Sea turtles swim so far;
The tide comes in; the tide goes out,
And, with it, all we are.

Morning

Rushing,
      red,
         ripe,

           Cardinals,
              raspberries,
                 currants.

                Singing,
                  woods,
                    filled,

                 Robins,
              bluejay
           bandits.

           Sparkling,
        leaves,
    light,

        Waking,
           flying,
             morning.

You

You are The Source of warmth and light;
You are The Risen Son;
You are The God made manifest;
You are The Joyous One.

You are The Way we learn to walk;
You are The Word sublime;
You are The Energy of life;
You are The Quantum Time.

You are The Yearning of each heart;
You are The Growing Soul;
You are The Parent of the world;
You are Our Only Goal.

Are You a Poet?

"I am a poet, too," you say;
Are you a poet, too, today?
Were you a poet yesterday?
What makes a poet anyway?

Do poet's dream and think in verse?
Do poets struggle to be terse?
Do poets try to words reverse,
Or are they simply just perverse?

Do poets always speak in rhymes,
Or do they only rhyme sometimes?
Do all their jingles ring like chimes,
And why must they use words like "climes?"

If you're a poet, it appears,
You have a different set of gears,
You hear with very different ears,
You stand out clearly from your peers.

If you're a poet, I would say,
You've found yourself the strangest way
To get through life, to work, to play,
To tell your tale, to laugh, to pray.

AN INVITATION TO THE DANCE

An Invitation

An invitation to the dance,
to sacred memories of grace,
to moments floating past your grasp,
to joys released somewhere in space.

An invitation to new life,
to dreams so ripe beyond the veil,
to all you came here to achieve,
to all you ever hoped to feel.

An invitation, that is all
that we can hope to have or be;
An invitation to sense truth,
to touch a heart, to set love free.

Beyond Time

Past the stars and numbered days,
Past our narrow, counting ways,
Past our fears that we will die,
Past defenses we all try,
Past our poor imaginings,
Past our finest gatherings,

God has set a world in place,

Far beyond our mortal space,
Far beyond our finite schemes,
Far beyond our petty dreams,
Far beyond what we can see,

God, past time, has set us free,

Free beyond this world apart,
Free within His loving heart.

Open to Life

Open to life...
Do you know what that means:
Open to God,
Open to dreams,
Open to being more than you seem,
Open like sunbeams dancing on streams.

Open to life...
Have you any idea
What it is like,
Love without fear,
Hopes broken apart, reshaped by light,
Born new each moment, born to new sight.

Open to life...
Are you ready to be
All that you are,
More than you see,
Open in heart and open in mind,
Open to life...
or lost in the blind.

Lost

Illusion's lost,
but what is found;
I search along
the unknown ground.

I listen to
a dear friend's tears,
A friend who's lost
remembered years.

I listen to
my love bereft,
For from his past,
there's little left.

I listen to
a young girl's pains,
As her young dreams
turn into chains.

I listen to
a lady lie,
As she clings to
a world gone by.

I listen to
my own soul's guide,
A soul who has
no place to hide.

I listen to
humanity,
Struggling, longing
to be free.

I listen as
I search the sky;
Illusion's lost,
and so am I.

The Past

Avoid the pain;
protect the past;
Then pain and past alone will last,
And strangle all your hopes and dreams,
And leave you with your fears and screams.

The past just like
a haunting ghost
Waits to seduce and trap its host,
And lure you toward what proves to be
Slow death for all your energy.

So when the past
invokes deep pain,
Embrace that pain and let it drain;
Release the past that holds you prey,
And live to love another day.

Tattered Love

A tattered piece
        of pink, plaid wool
            was all I had of love;

I clung to it;
        I cooed and cried;
            I hid it in my glove.

No matter where
        I had to go,
            I brought that rag with me;

I wore it down
        till it was gone,
            but still I wasn't free.

Inside my heart,
        I clung like moss
            to all the love I knew;

I found another
        tattered piece
            of love in someone new.

I clung again,
        as when a child,
            to ragged love, so torn,

That only through
        a miracle
            was I released, reborn;

Released from my
        impoverishment,
            from remnants of the past;

Reborn to God's pure mystery:
            abundant love,
               at last.

Touchstone

God is my yardstick,
My eyes and my ears;
With His abundance,
He fills up my years.

When I am narrow
In all I perceive,
He opens my heart,
So I can receive.

When, arrogantly,
I think I deserve,
He stomps on my ego;
He leads me to serve.

When, like memories,
I'm stuck in the past,
He moves me forward
With one painful blast.

When I am fearful,
Or when I don't trust,
He patiently waits
Till fears turn to dust.

He is forever
My sight and my sound;
I am eternal,
In His love, unbound.

Moving On

I've moved into a brand new space;
I've shed another skin;
I've left behind a bit more fear,
Some more unconscious sin.

"A cosmic bath," that's what one friend
Says life is all about;
If that be true, then I've been bathed;
Of that I have no doubt.

A cosmic light woke me before
The dawn broke on the hill,
A herald of a new found joy,
A heart that won't keep still.

A threadbare love left far behind,
In some far distant crib;
A lonely child remembered now,
No longer Adam's rib.

Autumn Bees

I always thought that I could be free,
Flying wild, like a late autumn bee,
Drunk on the nectar of rotting fruit,
Buzzing round in a heated pursuit.

I always thought there was something more,
Something brand new, some shiny new shore,
Something beyond the line of my trees,
Something beyond the warming noon breeze.

Always lost in my search for some prize,
I grew neither peaceful, strong, nor wise;
Buzzing round like the wild, frenzied bee,
I stung as I flew, careless, not free.

Freedom came only once I stood still,
Yielding my life to follow God's will,
Yielding my pride to grow in His ways,
Yielding my thoughts to pray and to praise.

Now days are pure joy; freedom is real;
Carefree, not careless, the way I feel;
Satisfied with the warming noon breeze,
Smiling, I watch the wild autumn bees.

We Are Playing

We are playing hide and seek:
You are bold and I am meek;
You are strong and I am weak;
We are playing hide and seek.

We are playing Jack and Jill:
You propel me up the hill;
You direct my scattered will;
We are playing Jack and Jill.

We are playing blind man's bluff:
You are somewhere in the rough;
You await me, loving, tough;
We are playing blind man's bluff.

We are playing show and tell:
You show me the ways I fell;
You tell me all will be well;
We are playing show and tell.

We are playing, stakes are high:
How to live and how to die;
How to love and not ask why;
We are playing, stakes are high.

How Slow I Walk

How slow I walk...
   My cross,
      heavy with sins
I would rather ignore,
      heavy with sins
I would rather forget,
      heavy with sins
I reject and regret.

How slow I learn...
   My cross,
      heavy with sins
Is my way to the Lord,
      heavy with sins
I must learn to accept,
      heavy with sins
He already forgave.

How slow I see...
   My cross,
      heavy with sins
He gave me as His gift,
      heavy with sins,
All His glory I lift,
      heavy with sins,
To my Lord who is light.

How slow, with Him,
   My cross
      becomes love...

Prostrate at the Feet of Jesus

Prostrate at the feet of Jesus,
Grateful for the cross I bear:
Balsa wood and sparkling cloud dust,
Lighter than the form I wear.

Prostrate at the feet of Jesus,
Awe-struck by the life I see,
Given to me, not deserving,
Simply my Lord loving me.

Prostrate at the feet of Jesus,
Graced beyond imagining,
Open-handed and receiving,
Each new gift, a song to sing.

Prostrate at the feet of Jesus
Joyous in His firmament,
Feeling safe within His mercy,
Captured by His light, God sent.

The Wounds of Jesus

I want to wash the wounds of Jesus
And bathe them in God's light;
I want to gently touch His children
And offer them new sight.

I want to heal the wounds of Jesus,
Wherever they may be;
To make manifest His gifts to me,
So others may be free.

I want to bear the wounds of Jesus,
To be awake and feel;
To know, through pain, the eternal joy
Of His abundant meal.

Dear Lord

Dear Lord, I'm here,
Among your flock,
A tiny chip,
Split from your rock.

Dear Lord, stand close
So others see
The inner path
From life to Thee.

Dear Lord, I pray,
I pray for grace,
To be prepared
To see your face.

The Face of God

I looked into the face of God,
And He looked back at me,
And what I saw reflected there
Was more than dreams could be.

I stood before the throne of God,
Resplendent, filled with light,
And found my soul, a glimmering
In His eternal sight.

I knelt before the crucifix,
Where death and life are one,
And found my true reality,
The Father in the Son.

I walked away, alone and free,
My visions as my guide,
The Spirit of the Holy Ghost,
The Triune God inside.

Friendship

Had dinner with a friend tonight —
I've known her quite awhile —
Long enough to see her grow,
to see her weep, and see her smile;
To see her courage to reach out,
and to see her fear take hold;
See her laugh, though reluctantly,
that she too must grow old.

What gentle comfort one may find
in friendship's lasting hold
Is much more comfort than one finds,
if I may be so bold,
In any other form of fun
or social interlude,
In any other search for truth
that one may have pursued.

Blue Moon

My dog and I,
We stood beneath
A moon so blue
It paled the sea,
A sky so bright,
It rivaled dawn,
The trees so hushed,
As awed as we,
My dog and I,
At half past three.

On such a night,
My son was born,
Twenty-seven
To count the years;
Beyond those years,
A gift to me:
His soul so bright,
It lights my life,
Like this rare moon
This blessed night.

Too Late

The Platt River calls me in early spring
to paint the sandhill crane
before it is too late,

Ten million years too late
to turn back history,

To protect the prehistoric uproar of migration,
the deafening celebration of rebirth,
the impenetrable promise of eternity;

Ten million years too late
to reclaim the waning waters
from the rapacious, driven carelessness
of creatures like me.

Have You Ever Stopped Awhile

Have you ever stopped awhile
   and watched the winter bark changing colors:
      morning light,
         snow fall,
            high noon and dusk,
   painting each ridge and knot,
      each gnarled imperfection,
         each graceful growing limb,
until by moonlight,
   you have witnessed every color of the rainbow,
      reflected in the stark bare dignity of trees.

Have you ever stopped awhile
   and listened to the forest greeting winter:
      a plaintive crackling in the air,
       a submissive branch
         scratching the earth,
           yielding to an insistent howling wind,
lest it snap and lose its life and be gathered up for kindling
   or raked away in early spring by the gardener
      into a careless pile of dead things.

Have you ever stopped awhile
   and felt the frozen forest floor:
      the roots of life
        pushing deeper,
         ever deeper,
           into the vital streams
             below the line of frost;
Above, the needle sharp air vibrating into every pore,
   demanding recognition and response.

Have you ever stopped awhile...

Questions to Rodin

Is the marble pushing out
While the sculptor pushes in?
Is the stone alive with hope,
Struggling to begin?

Does the sculptor, all alone,
Simply find and shape true form;
Or is form about to birth:
A head, a neck, an arm?

Though the chisel finds its space,
Is it guided by some force
That's been waiting for release
That charts the chiseler's course?

Dare the chiseler move too swift
Lest the marble not awake?
Dare the sculptor set the mark
When truth is what's at stake?

A Willing Shell

I let the past wash over me,
A willing shell washed by the sea;
The foaming surf weeps tears of life,
Moist memories of joys and strife.

I am the sand, made light by time;
Cleansed by the tide, I'm in my prime,
Reflecting facets of the way
We each can learn to be, to pray.

I'm finally a tiny grain
Made strong enough by love and pain
To take my place along the beach,
To write my poems, praise God, and teach.

LASER BEAMS

You Are Transparent

You are transparent
in the breath
that wakens me from tangled dreams,
in the song
of daybreak rising seashell pink and soft.

You are transparent
in the aromas
of coffee and strawberry jam
and wood smoke
escaping from last night's embers.

You are transparent
in smiles and hugs
and outright praise I receive
when Your gifts, in me,
bring comfort and light the way.

You are transparent
even in the roar of fear
smashing against my heart
like the stormy tides
of a determined sea.

You are transparent
in all I am
and in all I will become,
like a shimmering laser beam
echoing eternity.

Winter Morning

Ice dawning lures me out to play,
To photograph the world the way
The Lord is painting this fine day,
In rainbow crystals, glistening, gay.

A newfound glory in the grass:
Each tiny blade, a looking glass,
A mirror proud, reflecting light
That stays awhile, then melts from sight.

A soft staccato fills the air:
Across the field, the trees drip bare,
Releasing splendor held awhile,
Just long enough to tempt, beguile.

Just long enough to sense God's hand
Illuminating all the land,
Renewing joy, renewing hope,
As we seek faith and doubt and grope.

A shimmering, yet quite precise,
This is no careless roll of dice;
This is no happenstance, no quirk;
This is our loving Master's work.

At Herring Cove

I sat upon the stones of time;
They moved about and gave me space
To stretch my legs and reach around
And find a peaceful resting place.

Those stones they shimmered, nearly spoke;
They told tales of millennia,
Of how each rock had found its way
To this lone beach this sunlit day.

They shared their tale: they were content
To simply be where tides had drawn
Their energy, their history,
Their destiny from dawn to dawn.

I felt compelled to play with them,
Breath-taken by their age and might,
And wish no more for my time here
Than to be washed and shaped by light.

The Elephant

You always spoke about
killing the elephant:

"You can't kill an elephant with a pea-shooter," you'd say.

I always spoke about
seeing the elephant:

"One day, those six blind men will see the elephant," I'd say.

So we went our separate ways:

You,
to try to find a gun
big enough to kill the elephant;

And I,
to try to see clearer,
to remove the veils of blindness,
one by one...

Mother of Seven

Mother of seven,
Six I couldn't keep:
They went to heaven,
In God's house to sleep.

The one who lives here,
Borne by another,
A blessing, a son,
He calls me mother.

In God's precious love,
My children all met,
Tumbled and giggled,
Told me not to fret.

They played together —
So my son has told —
He and the others:
A blessing twofold.

Whatever seems lost
Returns in God's light,
Expanding our hearts
To see with God's sight.

Mother of seven,
The lesson is clear:
My children are safe;
I've nothing to fear.

To Robert Frost

My desert's black, like vulture's wings;
The sand, a buzzard's grey;
The clouds that promise some relief
Are pallid, thin, like whey.

The storm that stirs the desert dust
Is dry and fierce and cold;
Its whirling, biting, hissing arms,
A place where hope grows old.

My desert's black; my hope grown old;
The clouds, like vapor shields;
As year to year, a single drop
Is all their promise yields.

So little life can be sustained:
Forgotten seas gone dry;
Yet here and there, a cactus bloom
Defies the lifeless sky.

Grows strong, erect, yes, beautiful,
A miracle of grace;
Beyond the comforts of mirage,
God's light lives in this place.

The Sword of Jesus

God in my face at half past three,
God, Father Light, awakened me.

"I love you, child; I am well pleased;
I am the Lord; I set you free."

"Why do I please you; I'm bemused."
I was upset; I was confused.

He answered me, a steadfast voice:
"Because you love my son, of course;
You love His mother, tenderly;
Such love for them well pleases me."

"If you love me," I challenged still,
"Explain to me your perverse will:
Why did I have a mother who
Denied my soul 'ere I was two?"

"So you would know me as I Am,
And choose to be with me, I Am."

"Now, child," He went on unperturbed,
"Although you may be quite disturbed,
Stop fretting over what you've been;
Let go your life and let me in."

"I Am is all you are and see;
Relinquish all you try to be;
Let me do what I do so fine;
Accept, my child, that you are mine."

It Was You

They never told me it was You,
And I am not to blame
That I looked everywhere for truth
Before I knew Your name.

Inside the church, inside the home,
Inside a parent's heart,
Inside new love's seductive arms,
Inside each brand new start.

Inside the golden palace doors,
Inside the great old books,
I searched the faces of the world,
The saintly and the crooks.

I did the best that I could do —
I had my love to give —
I gave it to the things I knew,
The places where I live.

I gave it to the feeding crowds;
I gave it to a few
Who seemed like they could take my love
And know just what to do.

I gave my love; I did my best;
I did what I could do;
Yet all I did I did without
The joy of knowing You.

Without the joy of being free,
Without the truth of life,
I went through roles, as I was told,
A mother and a wife.

A teacher and a poet, too,
An artist and a friend,
A counselor and executive:
A list without an end.

They never told me it was You,
And so I went along
And did my thing, and searched my soul,
Not knowing what was wrong.

Today, I know my life is You;
I found out on my own;
I found out as I stumbled past
The empty roles I've known.

Today I know it's You I love,
That You know what to do
With all the love I have to give,
For that love comes from You.

I Took God at His Word

I took God at His Word,
at His Word:
How absurd!

I took God to my heart,
to my heart:
What a start!

I saw God in the light,
in the light:
What a sight!

I saw God in the dark,
in the dark:
Quite a spark!

I heard God in the wind,
in the wind:
"You have sinned!"

I heard God in my fear,
in my fear:
"I am here!"

I know God in my days,
in my days:
Give God praise!

I know God in my soul,
in my soul:
I am whole!

The Encounter

I've had a glimpse of heaven;
I've seen the light of God;
There's nothing now can keep me here
Except my Shepherd's rod,
Corralling me to stay the course,
Encounter Love in me,
Release that Love to do His work,
To set His children free.

The wisdom of the sages
Forbids our eyes to see
The Glory of the Living Truth,
Lest we prefer to flee
From earthbound mindless darkness
To where we consciously
Live openly, in full bathed Joy,
Through all eternity.

That wisdom, it burns through my heart:
A bleating, wounded lamb,
I thrash about uncomfortably,
Left here just as I am,
To do all that I'm called to do,
Though I now ache to be
Beyond the veil, where I have seen
My soul's home destiny.

Veiled Vibrations

Veiled vibrations
    barely separate
        night from day,
            life from death,

Hovering gently around us,
                waiting,

    until one day,
        we cross over,
            into their embrace,
                and find eternity.

Alone

I do not have a place to be,
No comfort zone, no reverie,
No warm embrace of memory,
No vague, familiar certainty.

I do not have a place to go,
No hidden dreams, no circus show,
No church that sets my heart aglow,
No rite for knowing what I know.

I do not have a place to hide,
No monuments to human pride,
No storehouse that I've set aside,
No fantasies for which I've lied.

I am alone and floating here
To do those things I hold most dear:
To serve, to love, to spread good cheer,
To live my life near free of fear;

To offer help where help is sought,
To heal the pain that fear has wrought,
To praise the Lord, my soul's home port,
To pass along what I've been taught.

Moon Shadows

Moon shadows on the silent snow:
The forest's winter majesty;
It matters not what plans we've made,
For God has planned this splendid show.

Moon shadows stretched across the field:
A barren oak made nobler still
Than ever on the brightest day
Its power and its presence wield.

Moon shadows in the heart of hope:
Foreshadowing of days to come,
When every step of blood sweat faith
Comes face to face with Love's full scope.

Moon shadows, dare we turn away,
Ignoring what we're being told:
That though we try to shape our fate,
Our fate is shaped by how we pray.

The Promise

The promise made so long ago,
A star that heralded its birth,
That promise made so long ago
Awaits a world to know its worth.

The promise made so long ago,
A faith-filled woman who said "Yes,"
The Lamb born to a world of pain,
That promise begs our willingness.

The promise made so long ago,
It lingers at the edge of night,
And gently tries to draw us near,
Revealing peace and joy and light.

The promise made so long ago,
Eternally, God's gift to man,
And, yet, we tremble at the dawn,
Reluctant to receive God's plan.

The promise made so long ago,
The invitation comes each year,
Enticing us to trust in Love,
To dare to walk away from fear.

The promise made so long ago,
A miracle that's offered free,
Received, embraced, within our souls,
Our hearts are healed, our eyes can see.

No Room

No room at the inn for the Babe to be born,
No room at the inn to welcome Him here,
Among merry makers and wayfaring thieves,
No room for God's Son, no room anywhere.

No room in the Temple for Him to teach Love,
No room in the Temple where He went to pray,
Among tribal Pharisees and hucksters' wares,
No room for Our Lord to show us The Way.

No room in the Forum for Him to bring Peace,
No room in the Forum for His Father's cause,
Among pagan powers afraid of His Truth,
No room in the Forum, just death on The Cross.

No room so much later, nowhere in this world,
No room at the inn filled with gamblers and fools,
No room in the Temple where laws measure faith,
No room in the Forum where larceny rules.

In this season of hope, let's make room in our hearts,
Make room for God's Word, make His Promise our goal,
Make room in our lives for the grace of His Love,
Make room for Our Savior down deep in our souls.

What Gift Is This?

What gift is this,
What miracle,
What chance to see anew
The meaning of our mortal lives,
Of all we feel and do?

        It is the gift that makes us one
        With all humanity;
        It is the gift that makes us one
        With God's eternity.

What light shines bright
Where all was dark;
What promise comes our way,
So we can sense divinity
Among us, now, this day?

        It is the light that clarifies,
        Beyond what we can see,
        That we, as Love personified,
        Are by this Love set free.

What truth is born;
What is revealed;
What lessons have we here
To set us on a path of peace
And move us past our fear?

        It is the truth that we are born,
        As Christ is born this day,
        To manifest God's presence here,
        In all we do and say.

Ben's Bus

Your servant came across the sea,
Forsaking home and memory,
To follow where he's called to be,
To live within Your Mystery.

Though bending freely to Your Will,
He senses he is mortal still,
And wonders, as he climbs the hill,
"Is this the path, or just a drill?"

For he who walks in heaven's grace,
A fleeting doubt is no disgrace;
And he's consoled within his space
By seeing God now face to face.

God's face revealed in simple ways:
A place to live; a job that pays;
A joyous heart that always prays;
A city bus to ease his days.

To John Milton

When I consider how my life's been spent
In careless running after gold,
In fear-filled yearning to be bold,
In clutching memories I couldn't hold,
Embracing lies I had been told;

When I consider how my time's been spent
In airports waiting for a plane,
In depots waiting for a train,
In deserts waiting for the rain,
Escaping from a world in pain;

When I consider how my love's been spent
In endless days of fantasy,
In glorifying pageantry,
In lover's arms to set me free,
Embellishing monotony;

When I consider what I've come to know:
That precious moments can't be bought,
That finding God cannot be taught,
That all I'll ever have or be
Is simply grace bestowed on me;

When I consider and I look ahead,
I see a world in disarray;
I see so many lose their way;
And I can only love and pray
And do my best from day to day.

Beginnings

This day began a thousand years ago or more:

Before my birth or memories;
Before my dreams and fantasies;
Before it mattered what I thought;
Before God's truth was all I sought.

This night began in some reverberating light:

"A bang," the physicists will say,
"Vibrations or a cosmic ray";
"The Word," theologians insist;
"The Slime," biologists persist.

This year began as every year began before:

An invitation to be born;
To greet with joy the promised dawn;
To grow new as new hopes unfold;
To live with faith a love that's bold.

This life began beyond all human reckoning:

Perhaps ten billion years ago;
Perhaps a universal flow;
Perhaps... perhaps... we struggle so;
Perhaps we'll see we need not know.

This Is My Life

This is my life:
It's a beautiful gift,
Filled with the joys
And the thanks which I lift
Up to my God
From whom all these gifts flow,
Up to my Lord
Who has taught me to grow.

This is my life:
What a glorious grace!
Lord as you lead,
I am led from disgrace,
Toward all you are,
Toward your purpose, your plan,
Toward all I am
Since you walked as a man.

ABOUT THE AUTHOR

Barbara Benjamin's first volume of poetry, *Through My Window,* was nominated for a Pulitzer Prize in 1989. Her poetry has also been published in *The Connecticut River Review* and *The Fairfield County Catholic* and has been featured in *Celebrate Your Divinity and Le Preuve Scientifique de l'Existence de Dieu,* by Orest Bedrij. Ms. Benjamin also paints and several of her watercolors and poems are the expression of a single inspiration, among them The Encounter, inspired by the same vision as the cover painting.

Ms. Benjamin is an Assistant Professor and faculty mentor for graduate students at Mercy College, Dobbs Ferry, NY, where she is the Associate Director of the Master of Science in Organizational Leadership Online. In 1996, before joining Mercy, she codeveloped, produced, and presented an eight-session multimedia leadership program for the National Technological University. The program was broadcast live to international corporations and to U.S. executive departments and government agencies on the NTU Satellite Network.

An international speaker, consultant, executive mentor, and retreat leader, Ms. Benjamin is also the founding director of Intuitive Discovery, Inc. In that capacity, she has designed and facilitated programs in leadership, human resources, innovation, and creative and spiritual development for Fortune 500 companies, nonprofit organizations and universities.

Ms. Benjamin's appearances include The Writer's Workshop in Geneva, Switzerland, and The Cenacle Center in Houston, Texas. In 1998, Ms. Benjamin codirected The Third Millennium Leadership Assembly in Campobello, New Brunswick, Canada.

Prior to that, Ms. Benjamin was an Assistant Superintendent of Schools in Connecticut and served on local, state, and federal committees on education and mental health.

Her other publications include *Leadership in the Interactive Age: A Skills Development Workbook* and the accompanying CDs, *The Leadership Lecture Series; The Case Study: Storytelling in the Industrial Age and Beyond;* and *A Modern Prayer Guide to St. Teresa of Avila's "Interior Castle."*

Ms. Benjamin loves to cook and she has also coauthored two cookbooks, *The Lenten Kitchen* and *The Advent Kitchen,* published by The Paulist Press.

Breinigsville, PA USA
23 October 2009
226362BV00001B/7/P